PROSPERITY

THROUGH

SERVICE

MERCEDES YOUNG

ISBN-13: 978-1-7356063-0-9

DEDICATION

∽᷈᷈᷈∾

This book is dedicated to my grandmother, Abuela Dolores in Panama, for her unwavering faith in me, for teaching me how to have strength, and being an example of perseverance.

Luci y Antonio

Spread the

flavor:

Menos

♥

FOREWORD

✍

I started my business out of my home after retiring from the Army. My journey was filled with potholes, roadblocks, and steep learning curves. For many Americans, starting a small business can be a daunting task and for those fortunate enough to move past the start-up phase, running a small business can be filled with daily challenges, sacrifices, and missteps. The art and science of small business ownership is often more difficult if you're a woman, especially for a woman of color. I admire those entrepreneurs who have managed to not just navigate the challenges, but have found ways to succeed and thrive as small business owners. I have even more admiration for those who make the time to pause and give back to help others to have a smoother ride to business success.

Over the years, I've witnessed many small businesses start and fail. I surmise that many of those businesses failed because businesses owners sometimes lack the knowledge and know-how to run a business to be profitable. Many business owners know their craft, but they sometimes lack the understanding of important business skills that will keep them out of trouble and help solidify their business in our modern-day economy.

2020 brought on new challenges for business owners. Those with great business instincts, business mentors, and a thorough understanding of how to operate their business during tough times are best positioned to navigate the tough waters of our current era. These small business owners will be positioned for solid business growth opportunities once we get through the challenges of 2020.

I've read lots of business books, attended classes, and sought advice from many who have walked the same journey. I have a strong desire to better understand and become more knowledgeable about running my own business. Business owners need experienced business owners to learn from. We need to hear the unfiltered truth regarding the highs and the lows.

It's just not often that I found owners who were willing to share the real struggles of their journey. Then I met Mercedes Young at a small business event in Tampa Bay. We discussed mentoring, formed a great relationship, and found ways that we could support each other in our respective journeys. Sometimes I wonder which of us is mentoring the other!

Mercedes Young is cut from different cloth. She not only runs her business, but she willingly makes the times to provide counsel and assist others with making their businesses better.

In this book, Mercedes shares a few of the challenges she's faced, the mistakes she's made, and the lessons she's learned. Her insights are invaluable. Her story is one of persistence and perseverance, and I feel fortunate to be able to call her my friend.

She wrote this book for small business owners to help them navigate through the journey from start-up to profitability. Mercedes Young takes pride in helping others succeed. She's humble and articulate, yet she's a force to be reckoned with. She's a trail blazer who helps women to believe that they can blaze their own trails. She helps men who are willing to listen. She has embarked on a journey to be the voice of black women in construction.

Read this book to better understand how to set yourself apart and create your own presence in the market. I highly recommend it!

As a retired Army officer and a small business owner focused on growing my business and helping others grow theirs, I consider this book a must read for anyone starting a new business or desiring to grow and position their business for the next level.

Brian Butler
President and CEO
Vistra Communications

TABLE OF CONTENTS

- The appeal of entrepreneurship
- What you know and don't know
- One of the reasons…

- One Towel
- Vivid
- Bringing the Heat

- Wake up
- Live your life by design, not default
- $2.3 Million Gone!

- Why, Thank You!
- You don't need to dominate the market, just your

percentage!
- Speed through mentorship

- Become a master

- Great connectors always come out on top
- Play the win/win game of life
- Core Values

- David, let me introduce you to my friend, Goliath
- Capacity and Capability
- Position yourself to Win

- My Bad
- How not to do it
- Transparency and Loyalty

- Respond with Alternatives
- I'm neither, but I'm more
- The Potential Power of, Yes

- Hey, Time, Listen up…
- Are you investing time or wasting it?
- Personal Inventory Time

- Right place at the right time
- Be Intentional
- Growth by Associations

- Don't get Bored, get Boards

Chapter 12: The Truth about Credit 85

INTRODUCTION

∽◦◦◦◦◦◦∾

I love what I do. I love helping business owners grow. I love helping my community. I love helping people free themselves from limiting beliefs. And I love encouraging budding entrepreneurs and seasoned business owners to serve others in order to find success.

I have long been a part of organizations and associations where I have met people who have benefited from my counsel. Most people who consult with me struggle with basic core values: loyalty, service orientation, and overall transparency. These values speak loudly about your approach to business.

As the owner of a surveying and engineering firm, I see building projects developed, literally, from the ground up. But I have met people who believe that cutting corners is okay. Recently, I met someone who felt that using the cheapest grass for a playground project is fine. That tells me a few things. First, it tells me that their children will not be playing at that playground. It tells me that "out of sight, out of mind" is a large part of how they view the world around them. It tells me that they are not open to the burden of creating a great product so they may receive the blessing of having pride in what they do. I also know I can't, in future, work with them.

If your company does not get repeat clients, maybe your style of doing business has room for growth. I've heard it said that it is easier to feed the chickens you know than to always be looking for new chicks. Every person you meet brings you potential growth, both tangible and intangible. I have built a multi-million-dollar business through the principles that I am bringing you in this book. Many other women who are dark-skinned and have an accent like I do struggle to break into and break through in their field. But if I have, then you can. I will share, candidly, what I have done and how I have done it. I will give you the secrets of my success that I have learned through decades of adversity and practical education. If you have ears, I invite you to hear.

My hope for this book is that it falls into the hands of someone who feels caught in the trap of how he or she has been labeled in the business community. I hope they are the hands of someone who has yet to reach their potential or realize that their potential is limitless. I hope they are the hands of someone who is willing to push back when a system is unfair and eagerly embrace opportunities when they appear.

Most of all, dear reader, I hope you are blessed to know that you are not alone. Others have gone before you and paved the way for your growth and success. I don't know of a book out there that will share the ins and outs of business ownership and management and be willing to reveal the good, the bad, and the ugly that happens behind the scenes. I hope that, for you, this is that book. I hope that I can help you see that there is a way over, under, and through the barriers that lie between you and your potential. And, I hope that, together, we can make your journey to success a more joyful one.

Chapter 1

THE STRUGGLE

‿ᔕᔕᔕᔕ‿

If you're anything like me, you've experienced a pressing urge to do more in your life. You have a desire to grow into something greater, more fulfilling, and more powerful. Maybe you feel like you are more driven than other people around you. If so, you likely feel drawn to be more independent and more in charge of the world around you.

For a long time, the way I've thought (and maybe you have, too) is: why be a sailor when I can be a captain? If I'm good enough to be the lead singer, why should I settle for singing backup? Ultimately, in our professional lives, we must ask the question: why be someone's employee and invest our time and talent to build someone else's dream when we can put that time and talent into building our own dream?

This is entrepreneurial thinking. This way of thinking has nothing to do with race, age, or economic status. However, once you actually start the process of entrepreneurship, all of those areas will come into play. Race, particularly, becomes an issue. It's presented to business owners in the disguise of one debilitating word: minority.

If three different people: a white woman, a white male, and a Hispanic woman, open a business, we would all be treated differently, starting with how we even incorporate. The limitations placed on certain businesses—those with minority status—can be simultaneously overwhelming and crushing. But there is help.

One of the reasons I wrote this book is because too many entrepreneurs don't know what they should know about developing their business. Not only does that slow their growth, but it can also limit their success. When I began, I was one of the new entrepreneurs who didn't know what I needed to know. I wish someone had taken the time to mentor me and show me the way.

Because I was alone in my journey, there were many detours and warning signs that I didn't recognize. I was so open to every opportunity, and yet, naïve to the business world. That can be a dangerous combination. It's a formula that begs people to take advantage of you. I knew I was vulnerable. If I thought someone could help me, I asked them every question I could. More times than I would like to recount, I got no answers.

The worst moments were when I asked a question that I desperately needed to know the answer to and the only response I got was, "Why don't you know that?" It's as if the expectation is that new, budding entrepreneurs are somehow born with the truth inside them. But how can we be? And if that's the expectation, how do we get the answers we need?

The answers must come from the people who have been there, who have walked the tough road, have banged into brick walls and found their way around, who have encountered hurdles and figured out how to climb over them. In this book, you will find the ways I have navigated around and through problems that entrepreneurs encounter every day. I will also reveal some issues that are unique to business owners who fall into a "minority" category and how to navigate around them. I don't have all the answers, but I have a unique perspective on specific keys to success for any business owner who is facing challenges that might seem impossible.

What I'm presenting to you can be applied across every field and discipline. I am presenting what I have found to be the most crucial areas where entrepreneurs need to overcome common and not-so-common problems. I want you to take this book and use it as a guide for how to position yourself to succeed. Let it become your manual, a roadmap to find the answers to some of the most foundational issues growing entrepreneurs face.

Whether you know it or not, in this book are the answers that you've been searching for. Should you implement what

I teach here and put these lessons into tangible strategies and actions, it can change the trajectory of your business, and perhaps, your family's success for generations to come.

Chapter 2

A LITTLE ABOUT ME

⁓⁓⁓

Growing up in Panama, there were seven people in our house. After my mother passed away at the age of 30, my grandmother raised my two younger brothers, my little sister, and me. My aunt and uncle lived with us, as well. We had one towel for all seven of us. As the fourth oldest in the house, I was fourth in line each day to bathe. That meant I was fourth to use the towel. We used that towel for a week. Every Monday, my grandmother put out the freshly-washed towel (no fabric softener, by the way) and after everyone took a shower, she put it outside on the clothesline. My whole childhood, I looked forward to earning my own money just to buy myself a towel.

At the age of 15, I got a job at a department store. I was ecstatic when I got my first paycheck. I immediately bought *my own towel*. I showed up at the house with my prize: a beach towel. You know, a towel longer than an average towel. I told my grandmother that I got paid, opened the plastic bag, and showed her my new towel. Without even thinking twice, she announced to the whole family that *we* (meaning the entire household) had a new towel! I was still fourth in line—with my own towel that I had just bought.

It was a pivotal moment. I realized that the only way I was going to be able to get a clean, dry towel when I needed one was to buy towels for everybody or to have a business that produced enough money to buy as many towels as I wanted. After that, producing enough revenue so I could own as many towels as I needed became an obsession.

Soon, I was moved to the city of Panama to go to school. I earned a scholarship to go to college, but I also had to work to get my bus pass money. The 10 cents I needed for the bus wasn't much, but it was more than my grandmother could help with. She was a widow, herself. My mother had passed. My father had left the country to move to the United States years before and we never heard from him again. I had to fend for myself. So, I went from house to house, rolling hair and painting nails to earn money.

I went to the University of Panama to study Psychology. At the age of twenty-two, I married an American soldier and moved to the US where I went back to college to study special education. I had my daughter when I was twenty-nine. So, what do you do when you have one child? You babysit other people's kids and charge a weekly fee. My first experience with a total "win-win." My baby had four permanent friends

6

and I built a business from home. As time went by, I obtained an insurance license and studied English as a second language at night to open new opportunities.

VIVID

About 20 years after my daughter was born, I was I was on my way back to Florida from a business trip from Puerto Rico. I was working for a company that performed 340B compliance audits and inventory services at the time. As I boarded the plane, it dawned on me that while I felt good about being a top performer for the company I was with, I should really be working that hard for myself. Even at forty-nine years old, I *felt* twenty-five. So, I started to look into it. I was always that employee who seemed to be doing the most. How much could I accomplish if I put that same energy into an enterprise of my own? I decided after that trip to go for it.

On October 10, 2016, I registered Vivid Consulting Group, LLC. *Now, I poured my energy and passion into delivering diverse services which, today can expand the nation through land surveying, safety supplies, corporate training, and the creation of curricula for long-distance learning.* After many ups and downs, we have twelve in-house employees and have served some of the largest design and construction firms in the nation, such as Jacobs Engineering Group, AECOM transportation, AECOM federal, HNTB, Langan, Suffolk Construction, SPP, Bouer Foundations, Hensel Phelps, The Beck Group, and many others. I started by creating an engineering firm and acquired a surveying company three years ago. We are now flying high as top producers in the safety supply services to hospitals and construction, as well. I personally continue to train the FQHCs (Federal Qualify Health Centers) nationwide, in addition to public speaking.

People have asked, "How does someone who ticks all the boxes of being disadvantaged in the marketplace (female, immigrant, "minority") become a successful entrepreneur and sustain that success? In this book, I'll tell you. But you have to be ready to hear it.

A self-cleaning stove cleans itself through heat. Once locked, it goes to its maximum heat output of 500 degrees. Just like the stove cleans itself, I'm about to clean your mindset from centuries of systemic, destructive thinking. I'm not going to beat around the bush. I'm going to give it to you straight. If you're ready for some burning truth, let's get started.

You told yourself that you were going to go to college, get educated, and get some experience under your belt. You did all of that. Remember when you were a new professional, when you got your first job and you realized that you were going to get paid salary instead of an hourly rate? You were so excited to make more than $50,000 per year as a new employee with a degree. Then, wow. After about three months you realized that all the projects with tight deadlines became yours. You've been getting to the office first and leaving last. Then, as you started to feel burned out from the grind, you did the calculations and realized that you have been netting about fifty cents per hour. Your boss loves you. You are the go-to person in your company.

Yet, you don't feel valued.

Then one day, one of your loved ones wakes you up to the fact that you have no life. The illusion is shattered. Your education, your profession, it has all fallen far short of your expectations. Now, you are asking, "What would my life be like if I worked this hard for myself?" Ah ha. There it is. The question that almost every professional asks at some point. But what are you going to do with the answer?

If you are a person who is committed to success, teachable, coachable, laser-focused, and unwavering in your commitments, then entrepreneurship is for you. Once you decide to move forward, it probably doesn't take long to come up with a business idea. So, you launch—you register a company with your state agency and get a FEIN number. Look at you! You have an identity now. You have taken a huge first step. Then, you start thinking: who do I market to? Old clients? My network? Maybe. But you don't have all those insurances, the years of experience and a team to back you up.

I'm here to help. Get ready, 'cause here we go...

Chapter 3

BE PRESENT

❧

As you are reading this book, I challenge you to *be present*. Get rid of distractions and annoyances. In fact, to get the most out of this book, go get a highlighter to mark parts that particularly speak to you. That will help you to be present as you read.

Live your life by design, not by default

You have to be clear on the life you want to create. If your desire for success isn't specific, or if it's attached to goals that are superficial, that desire will remain unfulfilled. Be clear and specific about what you really want, why you want it, and spend significant time asking yourself how you are going to get there. But, first, you have to know where you are going. The good news is, you probably already know or at least have a good idea.

Dreaming is free. So, when it comes to imagining a better life, visualizing your success and dream about your future, go for it!

Let's start with an exercise. Imagine yourself getting up in the morning, grabbing your cup of coffee or tea, and sitting in a front row seat to watch your neighbor's life. The children are running around, cursing at the parents, mom doesn't brush her teeth, dad forgets to put his tie on for the most important meeting of his life, the cat is hissing because the dog went to sleep in the cat bed, and so on. It's a house totally out of control. Well, some of us live our lives that way. And, what's worse is that we do it by default.

The truth is that we have a choice. We can create the life that we want to create. There is one key factor to recognize when trying to create a better life: every minute counts. Let us revisit the struggling family scenario. The kids learned to disrespect their parents from somebody, and the parents have allowed it to persist. The mom could brush her teeth as a matter of routine (like most of us do), the dad could have prepared for that meeting the night before and chosen his clothes carefully. The dog should have its own bed and be directed to use it. Developing routines that help a family flourish could be a way of life. They are simply habits.

When we hear stories of great people, we only hear the success. But I'm here to tell you that there is value in the journey of moving toward success. Right now, as you are in pursuit of the success you are seeking, your triumphs don't matter very much. As a matter of fact, I don't need to know about your triumphs. What I need to know is how you maneuver the detours and closed roads of life.

How do you manage difficult people and the funny looks they give you when they don't agree with you? Do you let them come between you and your goals? Right now would be a very good time to make a decision about the people in your life. What social circles are you in now? What social circles would you like to be in? It's very possible that your friends and family have never been where you are, trying to accomplish what you're trying to accomplish. So, if you are getting resistance from friends and family, what do you think about that? If you continue to listen to them, what do you think the results might be? Where will you be? How will it impact you? Do you think that will help you move toward the life you want?

Your associations are important. You've probably heard the adage: you are the total average of your five closest friends. If you take the character traits and success level of the five people you associate with most often, you are, most likely, at or near the average of those five. These associations can either hold you back or help you grow and move forward. The good news is that you can choose the people you surround yourself with. You have an opportunity to be a trail blazer. Seek out people who are present. Choose to be around people of strong character and high integrity who have achieved success and are willing to support your success. Make room for them in your life.

Now, you might have to stand up for your new associations to introduce them into your current groups. Ask for permission to bring someone with you to meetings, events, and outings. What's the worst that can happen? Most likely, if you ask to introduce someone new to a group, the answer will be yes. If your group reacts negatively, apologize for having been presumptuous, attend the meeting, and make sure that you make a positive and wonderful statement with your presence.

Another key aspect to being present is to be mindful of your finances. Only spend or invest in those things that will produce for you or your business. If going to the country club will help you to meet the decision-makers of the company that you want to engage with, then go to the country club. Make sure to be present, jovial, and vivid. Be a positive addition to the atmosphere. And whatever you do, keep your clothes on and don't get drunk. Memberships can be pricey, but they can be a great investment. Treat them as such. Don't waste the investment by behaving in a way that undermines your success.

For many people, their financial goals are tied to their career goals. You define these goals. Whether it's as a business owner or something else, visualize yourself in that career that fits your personality, promotes a product or service that you believe in, and then become the best ambassador that you know.

I have a heavy Spanish accent. There are times when I don't understand myself, and believe me, that is part of my charm. There are some groups and organizations that respond very positively to my cultural background, so I seek out events

14

and position myself as best as I can to connect with the right people as often as I can. Before the event, I make sure I know who will be there. I look at the previous year's roster, then I decide if my money and presence will benefit from being a part of that group or attending that event. Your biggest asset is you. Your charisma. Be present in the decisions you make about where you go and who you meet. It's well known in business that people have relationships and do business with the people they know, like, and trust.

How you spend your time is a critical component to growing your success. Many people have a goal to exercise more, but they often don't put it into action. But that is a very important goal. You are your greatest asset. You must exercise to maintain your health and have enough energy. Build the habit you need to reach that goal. Add to it. Do anything—park far from the places that you are going, walk while you talk on the phone, dance Zumba (that's what I do), drink lots of water. Is so easy to fall into obesity as a business owner because almost all meetings are around food. But you are in control. Control for those temptations. Eat a healthy meal before the event so that you won't be hungry. You make the decisions that determine your health, so make choices that feed your success.

Time, however, is the most important entity that you get to command. Tell time what to do. You get to decide what time you're going to wake up and everything else you do during the day. When you decide to be somewhere, that means that you have also decided not to be somewhere else. People ask me all the time, "How do you get everything done? How can you get so much accomplished in a day?" My answer is, "I tell time what to do."

I decided many years ago that I would not allow time to control me. When people say, "Time escapes me," or "I don't have enough time," I cringe. It drives me nuts to hear that. What I just heard them say is that they surrendered their control. Who does that? If something takes more time than what you anticipated, just shift. Move things around. But whatever you have determined needs to be done that day--get it done. If you need to shift your schedule around, communicate with the people that you committed to. Your phone has a calendar app. Make sure you're using it.

Create systems around time. A system is just an organized method to get things done. You can probably refine what you already do and create habits that will improve how you use your downtime. If you feel there aren't enough minutes in a day, get creative and think of how you can pull minutes from another area of your life to add to your productivity. Pair something active with something passive. Meditate while you shower or while you cook. Listen to audio trainings while you drive. Dust the furniture while you're on the phone. Have your tea or coffee while answering your emails.

Improving your habits and refining your systems is totally dependent on your behavior. Your behavior comes from the decision you make on how you will act. It's all about how you decide to act. When you were little, your parents probably told you something like, "When we go to the store, you better act right." They were telling you to choose to act in a way that doesn't cause chaos. As adults, we can choose to act in a way that diminishes drama and opens up our lives to improvements and even increase.

When you are in public, you can tell yourself, "I'm going to act right." Making conscious choices before you go out can increase your likelihood of success. What are you going to bring? How are you going to react to others? How are you going to behave? These are deliberate choices. Showing up on time for an event, acting kind toward others and demonstrating a willingness to serve are great decisions. We can plan to act a certain way. But we do have to be careful that our plans don't interfere with our ability to be present.

Planning ahead and putting thought into our preparation and expectations are positive behaviors. But once you are at the event or in the moment you have planned, your focus and attention should be on that event. Who is here? What are we trying to accomplish? How can I help? All the benefits of planning and all decisions you made to act with positive behaviors can disappear instantly if you allow yourself to lose focus. If you can't be fully in the moment or be present in conversations and focus on your reason for being where you are, you are not benefitting from being there.

Ultimately, you should be thinking about how you relate to your world in terms of the legacy you leave behind. When all is said and done, were you a person of integrity and someone who pursued growth and success? What will be said about you during your eulogy?

I have gone to funerals where they said things such as, "She was always optimistic," "He was always late," "She was a fashionista," or "he was my go-to person." How do you think people will remember you?

If you want to plan your funeral and dictate what's in your eulogy, you have that power. Be the eulogy that you would like to hear. Be kind, patient, and make sure your kids know that you love them unconditionally. Take the time to cultivate relationships. Spend time with friends and celebrate people. After all, the worst funeral is the one that few people show up to.

If we were to choose to live our lives as if our eulogy is being written based on each decision we make and each thing we do, we would probably be more present and diligent, striving to always do our best and live with integrity.

$2.3 Million Gone!

Sometimes, being present can be challenging. I had a business partner, a civil engineer who was going through a personal crisis. He decided, without my knowledge, to cancel all of our contracts. Without a single word to me, he cancelled agreements that would have resulted in 2.3 million dollars in business that year.

I remember where I was when it happened. It was noon and I was getting ready to take the stage as a guest speaker at Nova Southeastern University. My phone lit up to let me know a new email had arrived. I opened the phone and there it was. He was sending an email to all our clients, cancelling the contracts that we had. I took a deep breath. I refocused on where I was and why I was there. I was determined to be present for my audience. I told myself, "You are going to give them your best. These precious people are here to receive knowledge and wisdom." I stepped forward and walked to the stage.

After the speech, I returned backstage. I thought, "I did it." The audience had been engaged and received every word I had said. They responded warmly and enthusiastically. My husband hurried over to me and assured me that the audience didn't even notice that I had just experienced one of the most traumatic professional experiences of my life. After I left the venue, we went to my husband's office and I broke down and cried. I told him, "I don't know what I'm going to do." Thoughts of lawsuits ran through my head. Thoughts about the people that I know, the agencies that wasted their time selecting us as the right team for their projects. It was overwhelming. I went home and decided not to answer the phone for two weeks.

Through that experience, I became intimately familiar with high blood pressure, depression, and anxiety about the future. How do I show my face? I had to make a decision about how I would handle the fallout. I decided that I would not make up a story, but I would also not undermine his character—there was no need. He already had that covered through his own actions. I declared that, from that point on, I would only focus on the positive things that I wanted to create.

I got out of bed, called the clients, made appointments with them, and brought my new engineer with me. I will never forget the first meeting with a local agency that had given us a $1.3 million contract. They asked me what happened. I replied, "I only have 90 seconds to talk about it, and then after that I would like to introduce my new team member." I told them the truth---I didn't know why he did that. They acknowledged my tough position and expressed their respect for the way I handled the situation. They welcomed me to keep working with them. Another agency asked me if I would like them to ban him from working with them. Of course, I said no. I knew he had a family to take care of, as well. I moved on and acquired a surveying department. I leveraged the equipment that was part of that deal to get a $50,000 loan.

The following year, I added construction safety supply services to the company. I became a supplier for hard hats, eyes goggles, gloves, and various safety gear necessary for the construction field. I asked the manufacturer to share some sample products for display. With that, I created a shelf to display the products and applied for a retail certification. I passed the site inspection by showing proof that I had products for sale. I arranged my contract repayment schedule so that I could remain truthful to my 45-day commitment and sold the products with 15-day invoice payment remit so that I could turn around and pay the manufacturer well on time. It cost me nothing but some contacts and due diligence.

I could have let one of the most devastating experiences of my life—something that happened that was out of my control—become my excuse to stop growing. I could have lived in the past and said, "If only that engineer hadn't sabotaged my business, then I would have had success." Not only did I not allow that to happen, I didn't allow it to slow me down, either. I leveraged my solid professional relationships and found ways to strengthen them. I stayed present with my business, my clients, and my contracts. In a year that most owners would have just taken a loss, I turned a profit. Being present is one the best decisions you can ever make.

Chapter 4

Take Advantage of Being "Disadvantaged"

⌒∽⟊⟊∿⌒

Why, thank you!

I do not see myself as someone who needs a handout because of my ethnicity. When you come from a place where your skin color has never played a role, there is a different paradigm.

I can remember it as if it happened just yesterday. I had moved with my husband to Fayetteville, North Carolina. I was at a J.C. Penney's, looking at some beautiful scarves, when two elderly ladies moved aside. I smiled and let them know that they shouldn't have to move for my sake, that we could share the space. One of them muttered something to her friend. I distinctly heard the phrase, "that black lady."

At this point, I had no idea what they were talking about. I didn't have a concept of what "black" was. I looked them in the eye and told them, clearly, that I was not black. I said I'm "chocolate." The haughtiness of their body language didn't change. That disturbed me deeply, as did the fact that they said what they did right out loud, next to me, as if that were okay. They reacted to me as if I had a contagious disease.

I went home and related the incident to my husband. He clarified some things for me about what in the US is referred to as "race relations." Were we even a different race? Wow, was I in for a rude awakening.

The slights I would experience from certain people over the years due to my skin being a darker shade of brown did not keep me from focusing on the future. I chose to involve myself with people who were diverse, like me. I surrounded myself with people who valued me for me.

Over the years, I discovered that certain systems have been put in place to compensate for the fact that so many people still can't see past skin color when it comes to evaluating a person's professional capacity and value. For every social and professional slight that I have experienced due to skin color– many of which I am sure happened while I was not in the room– certain privileges have been granted to balance the scales.

Affirmative action policies resulted in placing criteria on many local government agencies for hiring personnel and contractors. I have no way to measure the impact that bigoted people have had on my professional growth, but I think we all can be certain that biases against people of color exist in certain arenas and do impact professional opportunities. Government agencies, so intricately connected to the political machines of our day, have been historically very impacted by prejudicial thinking.

So, the affirmative action hiring/contracting policies in place have created an opportunity for business owners like me. If the system allows me special privileges, it would be the height of foolishness and arrogance to turn them down. I'm going to take them!

Ultimately, I have made the best of and taken advantage of what I must work with. I was told by many of my mentors that, as a black Hispanic woman, I will be approached by white men with small companies to partner with, just so their company can qualify as minority status and gain access to contracts that they wouldn't be able to otherwise, and compete with the big companies.

Wow, was that ever true. I have been approached many times by male owners with that suggestion. Instead, I have adopted my own way of being that allows my reputation to surpass that distinction—a "minority" business owner—so I am perceived as a professional. I have always presented myself as a professional, not as a minority. To me, being called a "minority" is just like using the "N" word. How is it possible that anyone will accept that word to describe humans? It's purely negative. The word "diversity" is a much better choice. And, I make that point to anyone who calls me "minority." I want them to have an awareness.

You don't need to dominate the market, just dominate your percentage!

In my county, which is one of the largest counties in Florida, 876 companies are certified as "minority-owned businesses." Of those companies, only about 10% receive government contract business. From that 10%, I get 70% of it! On the surface, that seems unfair. But let's look more closely. It may be because I choose to support my community all the time. Instead of spending time on myself, I would rather be taking on projects that not many professionals are willing to, like cleaning buses. I also spend my spare time speaking to high school students about their future goals, serving food to people who are hungry, or teaching women how to present themselves in an interview.

Either way, I have a presence that cannot be ignored. And this is something you can do, too. Make yourself known in such a way that even when you're not at an event, people expect to see you. Join local organizations to make sure that you are involved in building the future of your city. All those organizations are public and people would love to have you there. Give your opinion in a way that serves people.

In addition, my company, Vivid Consulting, only provides land surveying, engineering and safety supply. We don't do everything. But I know plenty of other companies that can assist in addressing needs in our city. One of the values that Vivid Consulting provides is that we are a hub in a network of potential resources. I'm seen as a go-to person when there is a need. Being in that position is priceless.

Even though the "minority" percentage number is small, there are still a lot of businesses out there. I'm diligently working at every level of diversity in every area that we can imagine, making the term "minority" obsolete and officially become a business that represents "diversity." After all, what is minority anymore? Black? Latino? Female? Homosexual? Old? Non-white? Something is wrong with that terminology. The fact that someone would accept that term is repulsive to me. Everyone is, in a way, diverse from everyone else. But minor? Really?

Speed through Mentorship

As I said earlier, the different agencies require a level of experience that you can't obtain unless you have the certifications. I was going crazy when I started asking everyone in business, "How do I circumvent this process?" I did figure it out, and in fact, there are ways to do it. Today, I'll be sharing the most effective ones based on my experience.

Mentor Protégé' programs: The Small Business Administration (SBA) website will give you all the details of this program. It's free and a public source of information. There are different areas where this program can support you:

o   Guidance on internal business management systems, accounting, marketing, manufacturing, and strategic planning

27

o Financial assistance in the form of equity investments, loans, and bonding

o Assistance navigating federal contract bidding, acquisition, and performance process

o Education about international trade, strategic planning, and finding markets

o Business development, including strategy and identifying contracting and partnership opportunities

o General and administrative assistance, like human resource sharing or security clearance support

All of these are part of the public information from the Small Business Administration that you can apply to your business, a Federal institution created to support small businesses nationwide. What I found out was that the program makes the big companies look good and it gives them an advantage on selection for multi-million-dollar projects.

This concept can be applied to any type of business. Here's the concept: You go and find a company that provides the same services that you do, build a relationship with them, and ask to shadow them or be mentored by them. It could be in many areas of business, such as, how to bid on a project. In that case, you can shadow the proposal, or bidding department, or financials. I sent my accounting person to learn how to do construction accounting for four hours. We split the time to an hour per week.

You can also shadow the business developer or the technical department to learn how things are done for each client style. For example, there are some new software applications used to pull plans, reports, updates and even to submit your payments. You must also learn how to send proposals for projects. Something as simple as the right form can make or break your business (don't ask me how I know).

Be extremely specific about your company's needs. It may be all of the above or just some. Most companies are willing to support you, but all the effort may have to come from you. You must be attentive, open, and willing to learn.

Diversity and Inclusion programs: These are systemic programs designed to support the disparities of the business market. To create opportunities for small companies, every city conducts a survey and a study of the different types of businesses in the different market areas. For example: restaurants, retail stores, or construction trades that are owned either by women, blacks, Hispanics, Asians, and so on.

These studies are used to determine the percentage that will be required to add to each project that has county, city, state, or federal dollars involved (because it involves taxpayers' money). After these parameters are determined, the number per project is added. The challenge is that the numbers are always a single digit when the percentages are almost half or close enough to half. A good example would be the city of Tampa. In Tampa, the percentage of businesses that are owned by "minorities" (women, blacks, Hispanics, etc.) is 48%, but the percentage in construction for contracts of more than $300,000, just to pick an example, is 6% to 10 %. We have a company that has pushed that envelope to 27% (few exceptions). It was such an anomality that it made the local news.

Imagine that. The documents you will need will most likely will be the tax forms and the professional license that will attest for the services. The secret here is how to circumvent the experience that is required. You do that by bringing in professionals, partners or register directors who can prove at least a year of experience by providing an invoice from past performance.

After that, you must have a site dedicated for the business. This can be your garage. If you have to hold materials or goods, call a room in your home Suite A. The point is to prove that you have a designated place for business. The most important part is to prove that a 51% or larger stake of ownership is held by a qualified person of diversity. This person must be part of the daily operation and can't hold a job that performs those same services, as that would be a conflict of interest.

Once you have that in order, make sure to fill the appropriate documentation. Note: Don't leave any space on any document empty. If you don't have an answer, or the question doesn't pertain to your line of business, just fill the space with N/A or 0000. I bring this up because if you leave any space unfilled, it will not submit. All agencies that require documents will provide the support for free. It's important to know this because when you are starting or expanding your business, you want to be very careful about where you allocate your funds.

Even if you hired a support person for your certification, you must provide all the documents. It may be better to submit it yourself. Some would argue that it's better to have experts applying for you. Well, that's why the agency has a help desk.

Having these certifications does not assure you of any contracts: Let's be clear that having these certifications just allows you to play or participate in the bidding game. Now it's your job to develop your brand by letting your service be known by every prime company in town.

Also, no one will know you or advocate for you like you. A very crucial part of this is to know that as a small company with diversity certification, you get to participate in every team as long as you are honest, let them know, and sign an NDA (a non-disclosure agreement) with each team that you choose to go with. You can research public records for that agency to find out who had the contract before. You can even see the bid package that they submitted. That way, you can get to know the agency and learn about their preferred clients (although we're not supposed to have favorites).

If by any chance you do not get awarded, make sure to request a debrief. The best thing that can happen to you, though, is not to be selected at the beginning. That will give you an opportunity to learn. When you have a debrief, make sure to ask things like, What was I missing? What where you looking for? and What made the selection team choose the team they chose? Request support for growth and let them know your company goals. Make sure to bring the license, technical, or trade professional to the debrief.

Chapter 5

KUNG FU

~∞∞∞~

Become a Master

Too many people try to learn a little about everything and then wonder why their businesses are not doing well. Here's the answer: no one wants to hire a person who is a jack-of-all-trades.

When you need surgery, you don't go to someone certified in First Aid. When your car stops running, you don't want to send it to the guy who's constantly working on his car in his spare time. If that guy is any good, why is he still working on his car? You send it to a trusted mechanic, preferably one who is certified to work on the make and model of your car. In the same way, when someone wants to hire someone who does what you do, if you don't look like a specialist in that field, they'll hire someone else who is.

One of the things that I have learned from watching TED talks is that every presenter is a master of an area. They live and breathe that niche. I love the administrative and development part of business. In my head, I replay those conversations and ruminate on those ideas all day long. Let me share one of the most important pieces of business advice you will ever receive: stay in your lane. Doing so will help you guide your business and attract those things to you that align with what you most want to create.

I went to a meeting for a huge construction expansion at the Tampa International Airport. A lady who represented an assisted living facility stood up at one point and asked how she could get our business. The rest of us looked at each other. Was she at the wrong meeting? What did that have to do with construction? We weren't there to discuss human resource issues or worker benefits. Suddenly, none of us knew why she was there. After that, I thought, "Wow, what a waste of time."

Let's examine what was wrong with that scenario. She came to a construction meeting as a visitor asking us about assisted living. Everyone in this group was representing people who were able-bodied. Maybe an accident on the job would entitle someone to worker's compensation benefits, but disability and health benefits were not under any member's purview. The crowd was filled with top-notch professionals and constituted a large network. But even if they were inclined to do so, no one could figure out how to connect with her and what she needed.

Now, if you have ninja skills, you can market yourself in unwelcoming environments. She could have employed a wrap-around-the-room strategy. For example, when I go to a networking event, I start by meeting everyone at least three feet away from me from the right to the left. I take pictures, exchange business cards and ask to set up a future meeting. I make sure to arrive first and leave last with cell phone numbers, names of decision makers, and set appointments.

I look at networking opportunities very specifically: When I'm at an event, every minute at that event counts. That is my only chance to meet those people. In twenty-seven years of business development, this method has worked better for me than any other.

Master your area, be passionate, and learn all you can from experts in your area. Invest in conferences and go to every training at every conference. While there, look for ways to turn attention to you. Then be your brand.

With enough consistent exposure through being visibile at events and meetings in your community, your personal brand will be noticed. When people start attaching your visibility and your credibility to you, personally, as a professional, you will be regarded as a leader in your field.

If you are striving to be considered a subject matter expert and leader in your field, then you need to know if you have accomplished that goal. How will you know? You'll know when people call you—constantly—to ask for ways to acquire your services in that area. Until you are sought after by those who need your particular expertise or teaching the masses about your niche, you have not achieved Kung Fu.

In the US, we understand Kung Fu to be a martial arts mastery so powerful that moves are performed with such speed and grace that the moves invoke fear in the opponent. Certainly, that's true of the Kung Fu we have seen in movies and television. But in China, Kung Fu describes the process of studying, learning, and practicing. Specifically, Kung Fu depicts any set of skills that require patience, energy, and time to complete. It could be martial arts or it could be networking. Or, it could be studying the finer points of the niche you want to master.

Ultimately, it's the patience, energy, and time you decide to devote to study and practice in your business that will set you apart from your competition. No matter what barriers stand in your way, if you stay in your lane and devote the necessary focus to growing yourself as a business owner, you can achieve Kung Fu. The good news is that your competition will thin dramatically as you go, since few ever achieve Kung Fu.

Chapter 6

ENGAGEMENT

~∞∞∞~

My personal motto is: "Always in service." I use this phrase as a sign-off on my emails. I want to be known as someone who stands at the ready to be in service to others. Why? Because it's important to my business, my success, and my sense of purpose to be known as a connector—reaching out to people in order to connect with them for the purpose of positively impacting their lives. There are several tangible benefits to being a connector.

Great connectors always come out on top

In the arena of business, engaging with others is critical for every person who aspires to success. Engagement builds the relationships that create the win-win situations. How? Connecting from one human to another keeps you in a position of value, and this value transcends personal and cultural differences. It does not matter where you come from or what your cultural beliefs are. We can listen strategically to find the answers that create connectivity What do we have in common? Family? Foods? Children? Places? Hobbies? Charities?

All of these are things that connect us in one way or another. People all around the world love others and want to be loved and heard. Based on that premise alone, everyone you know is part of the puzzle of your life and you are a part of theirs. These are basic human interaction principles. If you aspire to connect meaningfully with others, tell yourself to reach out whenever the opportunity presents itself. Create an expectation within yourself that when someone comes into view, you will engage with them somehow. Whatever you tell yourself is your gift, the universe will prove it to you.

I was once at the Miami airport, reading a book about living in mastery, when someone next to me struck up a conversation. Early on, he asked me, "What do you do?"

I responded, "I help people connect."

I had just finished speaking those words when an African lady approached me in her native language to ask me to let her use my phone to call someone in Miami. As I gave her my phone, she gave it back and showed me a paper with a number. I figured that she wanted me to dial it. It was a Miami area code. I dialed and a man with a heavy accent answered the phone. I described the situation before me and found out that he was a relative of the lady. He asked me to please tell him which gate we were at and to keep the lady next to me. As I handed the phone to her, they spoke in their native language. He eventually showed up and was able to find her.

The man next to me nodded and said, "I see what you do."

I had declared that I was a connector for so many years that it had become natural for people to come to me when they needed to connect.

"Always in Service" has been my motto since I arrived in this country. It has attracted many needy people, many takers, and many givers into my life. The secret is figuring out who the takers and who are the givers are. Does everyone want to give and cooperate? No. But what if I know that, for me, the source of my giving or abundance never stops? Well, in that case, I don't have to worry about who takes and who gives. I give unconditionally, either way.

Now, that doesn't mean that I don't watch what I give, how much I give, and to whom I give it. Remember the instructions that say, "Put on your oxygen mask before you help someone else?" In my curious mind and childlike thinking, I contemplated the different ways I could hold my breath to help someone else. But physiologically, that just doesn't work. I once was in a relationship where I tried to help him without putting on my "mask" first. Without enough good oxygen, we both fell apart.

What does this mean? It means that you can't give from an unhealthy place. If you are in a place of scarcity, neglect, woundedness, and neediness, you need to limit how often and in what manner you give. Think about what that would look like. How are you supposed to serve and give when you haven't created what you need for yourself? That oxygen mask is a hard mask to keep on for a long period of time. It brings resentment because most of your time is not spent giving, it's spent taking.

I want you to listen to me here. You may have heard it said that giving so that you can gain is a positive thing. I'm here to tell you that it isn't. Giving in order to get is just a manipulative form of taking. If I'm giving but I'm neglecting myself, it's just like not putting my mask on. If I do that, I'm slowly dying.

Giving from a wounded place is very painful. In that situation, you will push yourself despite your beliefs and neglect your authentic self, and that hurts even more. After all, you cannot escape from yourself. Lastly—and this one is tough—if you are giving from a place of neediness, you have made a fatal move because you can become a slave to your master. The person that you help will probably find out your motives, your weak spots, and could easily take advantage of you.

"Always in service" will always serve you. There are foundational principals such as "give and you shall receive." My whole life has been a series of unusual blessings based on this axiom.

Recently, I lost a contract to a large infrastructure building company. It was worth almost three million dollars. Let me share how that served me. I decided to give a gift to five people I knew. I didn't know who, exactly, but I felt I needed to bless five people. So, early in the COVID-19 epidemic, I decided to buy 50 surgical masks to help protect some of our workers in the field from the virus. I opened the box and waited for people to ask me masks. Soon after, I was having a casual conversation with a friend from a foundation building company. He asked me if I knew where to get some masks. I told him I had some and he was welcome to come by the office to pick some up. The very next day, I received an order for 6,000 masks from that company.

I was pleasantly surprised, but because I was often a connector of people, it's not a stretch that this man saw me as a problem solver, too. Soon after, another coworker was talking about how her daughter needed to go to a presentation, but she didn't feel safe. I offered to meet her and bring some masks with me. I brought her daughter ten masks, and two days later, her uncle ordered 1,000 masks. My coworker's daughter followed up on that by making a comment to the Diversity Director from a leading regional cancer center. She gave my information to the Procurement Director who ordered 5,000 masks and 20,000 gowns. So, in addition to providing safety equipment for field workers, my company has expanded into providing safety equipment to hospitals. All because I wanted to give away a few masks.

While I was developing our chapter of NABWIC (National Association of Black Women in Construction), I was really struggling with my business. But now I know that the secret to receiving is actually to give. Not giving in order to gain, just giving to give. So, I put extra focus into developing this group. We became the largest chapter they have ever had, nationally, and my production went from $350,000 to $850,000 in one year. Give, and it shall be given unto you. Living a life of service becomes a life of receiving.

The Win-Win Game of Life

How do I play a win-win game in life? By working rigorously and being passionate about finding my own balance. I believe that we can have it all if we love everything and are attached to nothing. As we build our families (immediate and remote), we show them love. But we have to remember to show ourselves love as well. It could be something as simple as cooking what they like and what you like.

I remember when I had my self-love awakening. I was at the grocery store with the family and we went to the dairy aisle where I always buy everyone's favorite cheese. I know that my daughter loves Gouda and my son's favorite is Muenster. That day, I wondered to myself, "What's *my* favorite cheese?" I couldn't think of one. I had put myself and my preferences on the back burner for so long that I forgot. I stopped pushing the cart and asked my family members, "Do any of you know what my favorite cheese is?" I was upset with myself for allowing seventeen years of self-denial that I had been calling "love." Today, I buy my favorite cheese. It's Havarti with dill, and just in case you don't know, it's delicious!

As we experience people and places, we can learn to give and to have. Life is not a sport of exclusion. Contrary to the Olympics concept, everyone can have a medal. If we consider treating others as we would like to be treated, we can create a win-win attitude and way of being.

As a mother and Hispanic, I grew up teaching my children to eat three times a day. Over time and after many unpleasant dinners, I learned that not everyone is that hungry that often. But I wanted my kids to learn to consider time at the dinner table as an important time to share as a family. So, I asked them to sit at the table with all of us, even if they weren't eating. That was my win-win. I focused on what I really wanted out of our family dinners and gave them a choice in something that was less important.

In business, I have to make sure that my employees get what they want out of the time and skill they bring to the company. Some get financial bonuses and some get tuition reimbursement. Some want to bring their immigrant families to this country and we provide support for passport expenses and legal counsel. We all win, because they love and respect their positions at work.

I was managing a dispute among the field crews about which field radios would suit us better for what we do. Since I don't do that type of work, I asked for their ideas and asked them to do some research and text me the link to a product they would recommend. They went to town doing that homework. In fact, they agreed to a brand and distance frequency. However, they did not agree on the speaker capacity of the radios. One wanted a separate speaker and the rest felt that if the radio is of great quality, the speaker would be, too. I decided to purchase the same radio for everyone and a special speaker for the one who requested it. I listened to my employees, honored their requests, and they repay me with commitment to the company.

If we put our egos aside and think outside of the box, a win-win is possible in nearly every situation. Sometimes we need other people's opinions because our box is all we know. I know that in a capitalist system this can be a challenging concept because the system can become twisted in some corporate environments. If we only focus on monetary capital, then we can easily lose touch with the human side of business. We can start saying, "I will grow, I will be successful, I will have..." But do you hear the self-centeredness of that? On the other hand, teams can create a lot more. Together, we can serve faster and expand faster. Not only is cooperation possible, it is also peaceful and productive.

When it comes to teaming up with others, culture matters, size matters, and capacity and capability matter. As we look at the different services we provide, we have identified our target market. I always say, "No one can do it alone." I do not care how big, talented, or diverse we are. We need each other to accomplish big and great things. We can start by finding the niche in our business.

What do I mean by that? Find the places where you are unique. For example: I wear size four clothing. When I travel,

I shop for clothes in the parts of my city and the cities I go where the average population in that area wear size eight and up. I can almost always find an abundance of clothes on sale. The same goes for my business. There is a demand for minority, diversity, and inclusion in the construction and supply chain in all county, city, state, and federal projects. I choose, based on the makeup of my company, to target my clients by that needed criteria.

This strategy is successful for several reasons: (1) the rules and regulations are in place, (2) the demand is there, and (3) the support structure is there. As a business developer, I take a close look at the culture of different companies. Some are open to new, diverse, and demographically different people and processes. Some only work with the same people that they know, like, and trust. Others do the minimum in participation of diversity because of deeply-rooted belief systems.

Once you can identify these qualities, you must research your target clients and find out who they prefer to work with. We also need to ask ourselves: how do we approach these prime companies while honestly offering our services according to our capacities? Being a black or brown company owner is not enough. That program was created to create opportunities. Nevertheless, the quality of your services is what will speak for you and keep you in the services conversation. You can plan and create your very own win-win.

Core Values

Engagement based on the core values of loyalty, service orientation, and overall transparency always creates positive returns. How you engage will define the types of clients you have and whether you're still in business five years later. In Chapter 8, we'll talk about how to handle challenges. Adversity is a part of life. But adhering to core values is your protection so that even when things don't go your way, your reputation and ability to continue to do business in the future remains intact.

I adhere to these values because I am the face of my company. My integrity goes before me to every meeting. By holding strong to core values, disappointments and what should have been barriers to success can surprisingly turn into wins.

Chapter 7

SIZE MATTERS

~~~~

For new or budding entrepreneurs, one of the most challenging elements to growing a business is doing so in the wake of other, larger competition who seem to have all the advantages and appear better equipped to win. But even very small organizations can create a path to greater success in almost any field.

David, let me introduce you to my friend, Goliath

For most companies, growth and expansion is only possible when team members have built the skillsets needed to hone the company's niche or take on projects currently outside the team's scope. What that takes is experience. When we realize that, it's hard not to feel like a teenager again, when all the job postings for any jobs that pay well required experience in that area. We thought, how am I going to get the experience when no one will give me the opportunity to get the experience?

The simplest solution is to team up with the bigger players. I know, it sounds counterintuitive. These organizations are your competition, right? Well, have you thought about the fact that they might need you? After all, working with smaller companies is a great way for established companies to multiply their staff so they can take on a project or client that requires more manpower. If you have two and you bring your team on board to collaborate with another organization that has two, a doubled work force can tackle bigger projects with a shorter timeline.

Collaboration is also a good tactic in the long term for several reasons. If you are familiar with your competition, you can identify where they put their focus. If they are successful, they have a niche. Once you know what that is, you can focus on outperforming them in that niche or in looking for a niche in another area and becoming an expert in that area. It's a lot easier to win a bid or a contract if you can fairly identify for your prospect why you are uniquely suited to meet their needs over the competition.

Also, in this age of impersonal business management, getting to know the management of your competition puts you in the position, again, of being a connector within your field. Is someone from the other company looking for a new job? Well, you may know a colleague who is hiring. Is your competition dabbling in your niche, but they would really like to focus on another area? You might be able to direct them to tools or opportunities to grow that area of their business so they are less likely to take on work in your area. These are the kind of cooperative, collaborative behaviors that can turn your competition into your best referral source.

The key here, is not to be afraid of the larger, more established companies in your field. There is much more to gain than lose in offering an olive branch and letting them know that you're not a threat. If nothing else, building a working relationship with them will help you bounce back emotionally from times when they receive a contract or client that you wanted. You can be glad for them and move on. Only a scarcity mindset will have you believe that one project's client is the only client in the world. Staying upbeat and positive about your competition allows you to spend more energy and focus on finding your clients. There are plenty of fish in the sea.

If you don't see an organization in your field that's open to partnering, there are alternatives. Team members can seek out mentors and offer to be a protégé. Or, they can participate in an on-the-job training (OJT) program. By creating or plugging into these kinds of opportunities, team members can trade their willingness to take on menial tasks in exchange for on-the-job training. This way, you will acquire the experience necessary to grow and learn and the mentor or trainer can benefit from improved productivity while reducing labor costs.

I used these processes with great success to gain the experience necessary to qualify for the public certifications that I needed to participate in different projects. Now, four years later, I stand on my own credentials. But I also offer smaller companies the opportunity to work alongside me in order to support them and help them build experience. Working with smaller companies is a great way to multiply your staff. If you have two and you bring on board another two, now you are four.

Expanding Capacity and Capability

I once won a bid for a project that required very high-level equipment. I did not possess the equipment myself and it was specialized equipment that couldn't be leased. On top of that, I didn't have a staff member who had the skills to professionally perform the work, even if I had the equipment. So, I brought in a sub-contractor. The subcontractor not only had the necessary skills, he also had the equipment to complete the job.

Taking on a new job that expands the corporate blueprint can be a small risk. You may struggle to find the right personnel for the job. The planning and processes that need to be created to work outside your usual area of scope can take more effort to execute. But, in business, the big rewards are never reserved for those who play it safe. It's those business leaders who put themselves out on the edge a bit and challenge themselves to take on work outside their comfort zones that bring the most opportunity home with them.

Once, a large firm from the New York area that served JFK and La Guardia was trying to break into providing services at the other airports around the country. The company was proven with military contracts around the world. They had been providers for air bases in places like Saudi Arabia. But they couldn't get into the US airport market because the airport service industry, in particular, is managed by diverse families that have shown a strong preference for working with providers who represent the same level of diversity. Through my contacts in the community, I was able to make the introductions and help this company break through so that the folks who make the decisions on who can contract to provide airport services would consider this group.

This firm from New York took a risk pursuing business that others had walked away from because it appeared closed off to them. But there is always a way to break through. Persistence pays off and risks can be calculated. Their persistence cost them little, but it landed them the connections they needed to break through and expand.

Giants seem much larger from the ground. But if you can stand on someone's shoulders, you can look that giant in the eye. You would be amazed at how many people out there will gladly lift you up. You just need to have the determination to ask until you find the people willing to help.

Chapter 8

OVERCOMING CHALLENGES

‿⁂‿

We can't get away from experiencing challenges. Sometimes we overcome them, sometimes we don't. That's real life. What defines us is not always the challenges we overcome. Sometimes, we're defined by how we handle the losses.

My Bad

I remember my first big project. I was so excited to be part of the winning team. Little ole me playing with the big boys. I was in for the lesson of a lifetime. We were awarded the project and ready to go. The second week, I noticed that my key person was acting strangely. He was printing all the files on 11x17 paper and tapping his foot under the table nonstop for eight hours. He repeatedly took deep breaths and wasn't eating. I have the habit of looking at people's eyes when I talk with them. I noticed that his pupils were huge.

I asked him if he'd had an eye appointment because his eyes were dilated. He shifted the conversation, and the next day was the same thing. He could not be still. I notified all the employees that I would be doing a drug test after lunch. Would you believe that he left the building and never came back? I couldn't find a licensed person for two weeks. The project now depended on me to move forward, and it was a disaster. It was agonizing to see my company fall face first, even though I managed to get the project done. I called the main designers and project managers and begged for forgiveness. I was transparent about what had happened.

During that time, I found the accountant using my company time to look for other jobs, and after we hired a new accountant, he was caught stealing. All this was around the same time that my partner had betrayed the business and we nearly lost millions in contracts. But I was committed to clear the space with the amazing people who gave me an opportunity. I never played it off. I faced my mistakes. I openly acknowledged that I should have had a tighter rein on the people around me.

Every colleague and client I have ever had to go to with a *mea culpa* has been understanding. The reality is that they have all faced adversity, and often in the very same way. The moral of the story is that when you own your mistakes, you will bring back everyone's confidence—and often gain even more.

How Not to Do It

I entered a relationship with a major power company in the United States. They asked me to participate in a specific project and to become the new star of a national diversity success story. I invested time with the VP of that company, we went to dinner and spent time sharing the values of each of our companies. The VP stated that he would select my company to be part of the team. We spoke about our families and agreed to stay in touch via phone and emails.

After a good year of traveling to be the face of the diversity portion of the team, we submitted our proposal. As expected, we won the contract and were awarded as a team. This major company then changed their tune and asked me for an open bid proposal. It was obvious that they were opening the door for another company to perform my services. However, they never allowed my company to do a site visit for a project that was 47 miles of land survey work! Every company has to know the work that they are getting into. We were supposed to anticipate miles of labor with farms and subdivisions. Yet, the project manager never responded to any emails, phone calls, or any other method of communication.

The right order of events would be to sit down with the chosen team and negotiate the price to accommodate the budget that the client awarded. Ultimately, I didn't have an LOI (letter of intent) to protect myself from the devastating sequence of events. My company had known their requirements were strict, but we had purchased the right equipment for the project, trained for two months, and prepared our team as we should, only to found out that they gave the portion of the budget that had been allocated for the diversity participation to the companies that they knew, liked, and trusted.

The contract portion that legitimately belonged to my company started right away with another company. They had performed a bait-and-switch on their client who had expected a certain level of diversity. This has become a well-known tactic of big companies to trick their clients into believing that they will comply with the diversity targets and show every intention of bringing in a diverse team, only to fix it in favor of their usual teams later. This particular company has done it so many times now that they've developed a reputation across the nation for taking down smaller companies like mine in exactly this way.

I cried, kicked, and contacted the leaders of the many association that I belong to. The market is totally castrated by the typical pattern of this company. I didn't know what I didn't know. The most that I can hope for is to be reimbursed for my direct expenses, but nothing will make up for the time, energy, labor, the indirect expenses, and the burden this placed on my company.

This company is so immune to the consequences of their actions that the contract was never nullified. If that's not systemic bias, I don't know what is. If I were to have read a book like this, where someone warned me about the biases that exist in all fields of business, maybe I would thought to have had an LOI in place.

Take it from me; I don't care how much they wine you and dine you, get your LOI from the beginning. Not having one created devastating consequences. I had to close my surveying department because of this breach of contract with one of the biggest power design building companies in the country.

I did reach out to my VP contact and let him know how this affected us. I asked him, "What do I do, now?" He said to get rid of the employees and when I get a contract in the future I can call them back. He even offered me work on the next phase of the project (eight months later). But I knew something, he didn't. I knew that his company didn't have the contract for the next phase. Yet he was willing to offer something he didn't have just to pacify me. I was enraged at the disrespect that he was showing me. I reminded him of the fact that he had a job that morning, that his kids were set up for success, and that I might have to close my company and look for a job.

I later spoke with one of the leaders of the client's company and learned how they were tricked into believing that everything was fine. They were never told their diversity expectations weren't met. In retrospect, because I had developed a relationship with the competing company, I learned to develop the relationship with the client, as well. That served me in the end. But these were hard lessons learned.

Another Example of What Not to Do

A member of one of our associations shared with our group how she had lost a contract due to client dissatisfaction. The client was a major transportation company who had hired a cleaning company for the public transportation cleaning services. The agency contract implementation representative called the owner to let her know of the complaints that riders were sharing regarding the cleaning company's image. Riders found their workers intimidating. The owner went off on her, telling her that no one can tell her who to hire or how to dress. She felt that the complaints were based on racial bias. Twenty-four hours later, she lost a three-million-dollar contract and found herself replaced.

Soon after, our association member asked me to support her and contact some of my connections. I had to let her know that the way she handled that situation was not to her advantage. She had actively destroyed the relationship. I advised her in future to adhere to the contract. If the contract mentioned image or any other requirement—even race—then it should be complied with. After all, she signed it knowingly.

But going off on a client is not the way to go. She could have asked the client to give her some time to remedy the situation. She could have requested that the client please let her know what part of the contract explains those requirements. Most of the time, contracts are the only way to resolve disputes and differences. Even projecting an image and providing ethics training should be addressed in the contract. Research the last contractor who had that contract. Try to find out what performance strengths they had and what challenges they faced. Much of that information is public record when dealing with a government agency.

Sometimes, separating yourself from those who behave badly in the workplace is the best thing you can do. I once knew a woman who was fired for lying. She had told people that she was the owner of the company when she was just an employee. She reached out to me and asked me to call the authorities on her behalf. Instead, I told her, "I'm sorry, I would have fired you, too."

Transparency and Loyalty

I would like to take this opportunity to take the golden rule to a deeper level. We have always heard the saying that you "reap what you sow," or "do onto others as you would have done unto you." On the face of it, that sage advice is very basic. But applied well, it can lead to even greater growth and reward. Consider social mirror theory. Essentially, this theory states that we can't really see ourselves clearly until we take into consideration the viewpoint of others.

I believe that it's useful to call on that great gift of a mirror to see ourselves. I remember wondering why I attracted certain types of people into my life. I had some challenging experiences in business. I seemed to be attracting men (I work in a 99% male-dominated industry) who were disrespectful or demanding. After much soul searching, I realized that I had a distorted perspective about men in our field and that I was disrespectful in my thinking about them that was manifesting all over my space. I believed that men didn't see women as smart in business, but merely as sexual symbols. I also believed that men, in general, liked to trap women socially and politically so they could look superior.

Once I looked at my viewpoint honestly and accepted this painful and humiliating fact about my perspective, I shifted and realized that I attracted what I expected. I'm not saying that everybody has the capacity to accept this truth, but I will invite you to entertain the possibility that we attract what we believe and expect. Just like in a movie, there must be a valiant character who will be a hero; the character's inherent courage leads him to become that hero. If you always attract users or mean individuals, there could be a strong possibility that you have a "victim" mentality in your internal dialogue.

I know people who seem as though something is always being unfairly done to them. The air conditioning was delivered broken. The coffee at the restaurant was served cold. The food is always disappointing. Their children ignore them. Their cat is moody. Just an incredible sequence of events. If they didn't have bad luck, they'd have no luck at all. You will recognize them because they don't keep long-term friends. I notice that these individuals are committed to having the victim conversation with others to attract attention. Consequently, they go through life believing that bad things always happen to them—and inevitably, they do.

On the other hand, if you expect great things, great things will happen. Even when it looks impossible, God moves in mysterious ways to make it great. I have an amazing husband—a very peaceful soul. He is loving, nurturing, caring, kind, giving, and powerful. I had to look at myself and shift away from the drama, the love-seeking behaviors, and my tendency to procure peace at all costs. After months of working diligently on detoxing from victims in my life (because I was a rescuer), he came into my life.

Transparency starts with self. Take a look in the mirror of your soul and call out those things about yourself that you would like to work on. Thinking about my future eulogy works for me. It keeps me alert to how others perceive me, even though I may never hear it. (But, who knows… I might!) Be loyal to your buddy. Your body, your health, and your mind are your buddy. You should not treat your buddy badly. Give yourselves the advice that you would give to your child. You won't, or shouldn't, mislead your child, so don't lie to yourself. When you constantly excuse your own actions, it's because you're being disloyal to yourself. The number of mothers who still use the excuse of baby fat after their kid is fifteen years old(!) is alarming too me. Some women buy shoes or clothing and then hide try to hide it from their husbands. Why would you do that? If you're perpetuating a lack of transparency and disloyalty to yourself and each other in this, the closest of your relationships, then guess what? He's lying to you, too. Now, that is a mirror. It reflects exactly what's in front of it.

The concept of the golden rule is very real, but don't just think of it in a passive manner. It can be actively pursued with powerful effect, as well. I once decided to take my safety supply department to the next level. I ordered construction sunglasses, sun block, and chopsticks for the construction workers. I went to a job site in a cold winter day and shared fifty of them with the field workers. I can't tell you how many contracts came out of that simple act.

Once we understand the power of the golden rule and mirror theory, we open our eyes to opportunities to create goodwill and invite success. But this kind of success can only continue if we are transparent to others and loyal to others as well as ourselves.

Chapter 9

NEVER SAY *NO*

One of the challenges in staying authentic and keeping your integrity as a business owner is being aware of your limitations. In order to keep our reputation intact, we don't ever want to say yes to something we might not be able to fulfill on, right? Well, when it comes to people, I would suggest that we should never say *no*.

Finding alternatives

As we go through life, we meet many people and businesses. Make it your business to be present with people. Find out what they do, their niche, areas of service they provide, and more. As you decide to enhance your territory, make sure to learn about other services just for the sake of connecting. You can help so many people around you succeed if you just pay attention and are willing to be a hub for connecting other people to each other.

Now, a word of warning: don't try to do everything and be the connector of everyone. I have never seen a company do everything; I don't care how big or strong they are. Everybody needs somebody. When people think of you, it should bring a smile or a positive feeling to their heart. Sometimes, to make sure that happens, we need to reach out to others for partnership and support.

The idea is to make every minute count. Be intentional with your time at the dry cleaner's, the doctor's office, the pharmacy, and so on. There is no *no*. There is a philosophical principle that essentially says, "If you can imagine it, it can exist." If you open yourself up to the possibility of *yes*, and you can imagine yourself fulfilling on that *yes*, then you are likely to find a way to fulfill on it.

I make it my business to attach the services they provide to the names of the people I meet and I include that in my phone contacts. It's very unlikely that I don't know someone who can connect with another contact for one reason or another. I have found that if I'm centered on serving others, then the service contracts will come to me. That was the secret to my involvement with the National Association for Black Woman in Construction. The more I promoted the other ladies' businesses, the more business came to me.

I'm neither, but I'm more

I'm neither a surveyor nor an engineer, but I own a surveying and engineering company! Finding my sweet spot in the world of business wasn't difficult. Once I learned that most professionals (engineers, professional surveyors, and even doctors) did not have a single hour of their education in business development, I was in business. I get to be the one who brings the business to the professionals. Did you know that business developers make more money than professional engineers and license surveyors? Because without the contracts there are no companies and no work for these professionals.

Operating in this area has made me a really passionate connector. I love to wine and dine while I travel and get to negotiate contracts. I'm a connector; if I can't do it, I'll find you someone who can. By doing so, I become valuable to both parties.

But in order to be good at being a connector, you must have some powerful conversations with yourself about your worth, your visceral energy, and your capacity to deliver. Nothing will hold you back as much as yourself. Stop saying *no* to yourself. Stop believing the lies you've been told about who you are. If you are a minority, stop agreeing with that label. A minority is the definition of something small, minute, or smaller than. It's a degrading word that doesn't fit your human potential.

The Potential Power of Saying *Yes*

When you say *yes*, you open yourself up for more business, more connections, more confidence, more clients, more happiness, and more of most everything.

The word *no* doesn't leave room for any options. The word *no* brings an energy of being at the end, of things being finished, over. There is no space, nowhere to go to after a *no*. Instead, I invite you to say, "Tell me more." That way you leave open the possibility of learning, of growing, and discovering how you might be able to serve.

I was watching *Shark Tank* one night and Kevin O'Leary (Mr. Wonderful) asked an entrepreneur contestant how many orders he could fill, and he said that he didn't take many because he didn't have the capacity. Mr. Wonderful let him have it. He said, "The problem that you have is that you don't have enough orders." He went on to add that it's better to have so much that you don't know what to do—you can always fix that.

I'm not suggesting that you become an irresponsible *yes* person. Simply keep in mind a spirit of service. When you know you can't do something you're being asked to do, keep asking questions (Tell me more...) until you find something you can say yes to or another way to help. Do you know how a leader becomes very creative, how they develop out-of-the-box thinking to come up with new ways to doing something? That leader says *yes* at key moments.

As an example, I remember when bottled water entered the marketplace. Everyone had access to tap water. It was considered a crazy notion at the time to bottle and sell something people already had access to for free. Crazy as it sounded to many, the product was a success. Then, a few decades later, the vitamin companies teamed up with the bottled water companies, and voilà! We can now buy vitamin water.

My point is that we should at least entertain the possibility that we can grow faster and also be authentic. Most new developments come from the basis of something else already created. You have heard the saying, "There is nothing new under the sun." Well, if we get in the habit of saying *yes* or being open to new opportunities, then the sky is the limit!

I remember listening to certain musical genres when they were uniform. Everyone had a favorite in that genre and each group of people only listened to their favorite genres. Now we have crossovers: reggae with ballads, salsa with rock, and so on. We even have Portuguese with Hungu. That is a very unique and great mix—at least it is, if you're open. Saying *yes* opens you to stretch the limits of your own box, to think bigger.

You should ask yourself: How do I make this happen? Just asking the question puts you on a quest. That's how I became the coordinator of the logistics of my company. I Googled and researched so much that I joined the surveying association in my community, attended engineering and planning meetings, and became involved in the city projections. That way, I'm always in the know and with a good business ear. You can come up with new opportunities if you open yourself up to new processes and groups. Create rules for yourself, such as, "If you are within three feet of me, we will connect." This rule has served me well through the years. Of course, when social distancing is required, it's six feet, but you get the point.

A book I read years ago, when I was at a different place in my life, inspired me to become more of a "SI" (supportive influencer) person. So, to become that supportive influencer I imagined myself becoming, I decided that I had to say *yes* to everything without even questioning what I was saying *yes* to. But there was a danger in that. When you say *yes* without asking any questions, you are giving yourself away for free. We need to be able to say *yes*, but we need say it while still valuing ourselves and our time.

As I look at where I am today, I realize that once I knew I was capable and believed in myself, I began to process information differently. Now, no one can make me do anything I don't want to do. So, when I choose to say *yes* to the many possibilities before me, it does not take away from me. When I say *yes*, I mean it because I want to do it. I can have confidence that I am going to give it my best and go for it with all my might.

It's also important to note that you should only say *yes* to those things that you know you can include in your timeline—things that you will give time and dedication to. I could not tell you how many people I know who say *yes* to everything and then do nothing. I am thinking of one woman in particular. The amazing part of this was that she was well known for a lack of integrity. Several people had voiced the opinion along the lines of, 'Sure, she says *yes*, but she doesn't mean anything by it.' So, I asked these people what they meant by that. They said, "Well, she'll say 'yes,' but then she won't do anything about it. She has a reputation of not being good for her word."

That is not what you want to be known for. When you say *yes*, make it a heartfelt commitment. There are many people who call me to ask for things that I'm capable of doing, but I take into consideration the energy and effort that it would require. I truly believe that anything is possible if you set your mind to it and if you are open to creating it. The real question, though, is how much time and energy you are willing to dedicate to it.

So, expect to say *yes* when called on to serve others, but before you do, make sure that you have the time and energy to commit. If not, be honest. Say, "I would love to help, but I don't have the bandwidth right now. If you still have a need in the next few weeks, let me know and I will check again. In the meantime, if you want me to try to connect you with someone who can help, I can keep my eyes open."

Sometimes, we are asked to help in ways that are just outside our area of ability. Again, be honest. "I would love to help, but I don't think I'm the right person to help with this. But I might know someone who is. Would you like me to reach out to a few people on your behalf?" Sometimes, being honest about what you can't do or offering to advocate for someone you can't help is actually a *huge* help. You can show genuine compassion by just being present to their need and taking a few minutes to see if you can, realistically, help them.

Being in service to others is about being open enough to say *yes*, even if it hasn't been your first impulse. But to be a true help to others, we need to have the esteem and confidence it takes to make meaningful contributions. For many entrepreneurs, confidence is something that must develop over time and through experience. But, you will have many more positive, productive experiences if you say *yes* more often!

Chapter 10

TELL TIME WHAT TO DO

∽ⁿⁿⁿ∽

Hey, Time… Listen up!

I tell time what to do. I'm not being arrogant when I say that. Whether you know it or not, you tell time what to do, too, and I'll prove it. If you were at the mall for five hours on a Tuesday afternoon, you chose to be there. You told time, "For the next five hours, I'm going to the mall." I tell time what to do when I'm getting out of bed, when I go to the office, etc. I want to share my experience on when I took control of time and how it dawned on me that we all tell time what to do.

I was leading a strategic planning development session and to complete an exercise, our team had four hours to create a play using a number of characters. Almost no one in the group recognized these characters, and we had to learn the characters, imitate them, and impersonate them from a deep sense of ownership of the character.

71

We took the instructions and delegated every part of the process, all the way down to who would research the characters and study reviews about them: what each character wore, how they walked, how they expressed themselves, everything we could find out about them. We were to designate a timekeeper. We named him *Time*. No emotions, no opinions, or filters. Just *Time*. As the group scrambled to make all this happen, we would call out, "Time?" *Time* answered with just that—the time. That's when it hit me: "I tell time what to do." It almost felt like I had power over everything.

After that awakening, I decided never to complain about time again. I dedicate time to walking, strategizing, relaxing, people, and so on. It is amazing the number of people who walk around defeated, having given over their power over their own time while complaining about being victims of time, saying, "I don't have enough time."

What? Everyone is given the same twenty-four hours every day. How is it that you don't have enough time?

It's not as though I don't understand the feeling. I do. Feeling like you don't have enough time is a very impotent feeling, like there is so much more you could do if you just had more time. Even so, aren't you choosing to stay longer in the bathroom, on the phone, in the kitchen, or at the office? Be present in the moment you're in and resist the impulse to think about the next minute. Do your best in *this* moment. Right now. Do all you can. Just do it.

The worst one is, "Time escapes me."

What is this? Water between our fingers? I actually believe that this is an attempt to dodge responsibility.

You know how you can be having tea with a girlfriend and the conversation is so good and the gossip is juicy, you feel the sense of time passing, so you look at the time and realize that it's time to go, but then you say, "I can stay ten more minutes."

A-ha! You just told time what to do. You chose to stay with you friend, so if you say later that time got away from you, you're not being true to your word. It's pretty simple. You have choices, and that's a beautiful thing. You just have to be able to manage those choices.

Notice that when you get invited to an event, it has a start time and an end time. For those who choose to stay beyond the end time (making a choice with their time) new things come, too. So, if we lived in a truly honest society, you would be able to tell your children, "The reason I picked you up late is because I chose to do something else with my time." Would you say that? Of course, not. That's not nice. Who says that? Nevertheless, that's still the message you're sending. In such an honest society, people would ask you, "What were you doing that was more important than me?" In the real world, the answer is a dishonest, "Time escaped me," or "I lost track of time." Why can't we tell the truth?

Before I started telling time what to do, whenever I was running late to pick up my children, I used to tell them, "I was making money to give you the lifestyle that you get to live." They looked at me and said, "Okay, Mommy," but their faces told me the truth. I was making them less important.

Blaming time for our own shortcomings is a very "victimized" way of looking at life. Regardless of whether you're tracking it with a $10.00 watch or the latest iPhone, time is a resource just like money that you get to boss around. Plants and animals are at the mercy of time. Trees have to wait for rain. Animal predators wander until they stumble across their prey. Plants and animals don't have character traits like drive, passion, or ambition. They lack the capacity to take conscious ownership of the situations they're in. These traits are among the privileges of being human and provide you with the ability to take control of your life, so don't give that up. You have the human privilege of being able to assert leadership over time, so use it. It's so easy to blame others for everything that we think happens to us, but really, let's own this. Tell your time what to do from a place of responsibility.

Are you investing time or wasting it?

Your choices dictate how you will spend your time. Some people *invest* their time, some people *waste* their time. Living a conscious life involves what we do with every minute. When I first joined Mary Kay cosmetics, they taught us to have a "power hour" at the beginning of the day. That hour would set the tone for the rest of it. I remember thinking that I needed to exercise, make coffee or just run around doing things. Pretty soon I realized that when I started my day like a nut, I had a nutty day. I started to investigate ways to control my running thoughts and high level of energy, and I decided to be quiet and meditate.

Wow, that was the best investment I ever made in myself. It controls my pulse, my nerves, my thoughts (I get my thoughts in order). After the first thirty minutes, I was ready to think straight and produce more. I was able to take care of my agenda, and the most important part, I was determined not to answer calls, emails or respond to any requests during that time. Detaching like that from the rush-rush pace of the world will do wonders for you.

I love to cook, so I make a hot breakfast for my family every day. I love to freshen the flowers, put new wax on the potpourri, play meditation music throughout the house and cook oatmeal or bake first thing in the morning, investing in myself and the people I love. I've also developed the habit of calling three people every morning to let them know that I think of them. These habits put me in the spirit of service. They don't have to answer the phone. I just want them to know that they matter. Remember: everybody matters.

Your presence is an investment in your life, your family, and your business. We must be mindful of where we take ourselves, meaning that every move should be intentional. When I go to a grocery store, it's to look for things or buy things that will nurture me, my loved ones, or the people around me. When I shop anywhere, I pay attention to brand names so I can choose to where I want to place my money.

I have friends who have asked me for money for things that I know won't be good for them, such as cigarettes. Sorry, I won't participate on that. I care for people too much. I have been in places where my presence has been requested, and when I get there, I realize that it's a one-way street and I leave. If I can't give, I won't take. Wasting presence can be a crazy thing, because you can never recover that.

I remember going to an event I had been invited to, and when I got there, they were bashing men. I told my girlfriend that I had to leave. She fallowed me and asked me what was wrong. I told her that I love men, that I could not participate, and that I would be going home to my man.

Even people taking pictures with you can create the wrong influence. I own a business. I'm into policies, not politics. I could not tell you the number of politicians who ask me for support, whether it be financial or with the associations that I belong to. I won't do it because I'm in "service to all." If you want to bank on the lifespan of your business, get caught up in politics. The political parties change every four years. Are you open to rebuilding your business every four years? Now, if the conversation is to support policies that will benefit the majority that's different. Just be mindful of what you do to get where you want to go. Ask yourself, will this event bring me closer to my goal, help me to grow, or just entertain me? If you are looking for entertainment you should go to the movies, to plays, or the circus, just choose the venue where the people there are where you want to be.

I want you to take a moment and write about how important it is to value your time.

- How much time do you watch TV?

- How much time do you spend playing games on your phone?

- How much time have you devoted to being present with your family?

- How much time do you spend pursuing the hobbies and passions that make you happy?

If you're spending too much time watching TV, you're wasting it. If you spend too much time doing things you don't like to do, you're probably angry all the time. Be your own master. Take control of your own environment. Don't allow time to tell you what to do. You tell time what to do.

Chapter 11

WHY ARE YOU HERE?

~ഗ്ഗ്ഗ~

Right place at the right time

The importance of being where you should be at the right time can't be underestimated. Being at the right place at the right time is often the key to creating huge momentum that works to your advantage.

Remember that meeting at the airport where the woman who worked in the assisted living field was there and we all wondered why? She's an example of being in the *wrong* place at the right time. Now, even if I had taken her card, I don't have the confidence to recommend her because I don't think she understands how to run her business. Timing is important and is rarely within our control. But business owners should know that being in the right place is completely within our control. Perhaps the lady at that meeting didn't do her research. Maybe she just felt like she had time to waste. Either scenario means that she is likely unprepared and poorly managed in her business.

There is a common business practice that never fails to surprise me. It happens all the time. We go to a marketing event and see people randomly passing out their business card. When they present me with a card, I recoil as if they've thrown a dagger at me. In that moment, I'm thinking, "Why don't you just be intentional and share what you do with gusto and energy to the point that people can't wait to *ask you* for your business card?"

When people see you walk into a room, they should want to get to know you and find out what you do and where you're going. They shouldn't feel assaulted by your presence. They should feel like they made a connection with you. When you leave their presence, they should be able to tell everyone else what you do.

Be Intentional

In our current business climate, we are inundated with distractions and disruptions. No one is immune. It's easy to get off task and then only passively get back on task. But passive activity doesn't bring powerful results. To achieve the results we need, we must be intentional. To be intentional, you need to ask yourself the following questions about where you go and what you do:

- If I go there, what will I do? Do I have a strategy?

- How many people do I need to meet, and who, specifically, should I try to meet?

- What do I want to accomplish by going there, or what can I accomplish while I am there?

- What solutions can I provide to the people there? How can I create a "win-win" for others?

- Who do I want to talk to? And, about what? What's in it for them?

- How long should I be there?

- Is it worth my time?

Plan for success at every event by having a strategy. For a networking event, I have found that a "wrap around the room strategy" works best. This is a simple strategy where you walk through the room and speak to everyone who is within three feet of you as you go. Offer business cards only to those people who ask for them. Ideally, you should arrive earlier than the average guest and stay long enough to be one of the last to leave. You'll find that the most committed connectors stay to the end. There is nothing more valuable to a connector than finding another connector!

Ultimately, you will want to evaluate what tangible results you expect from being in that place at that time. Will you set meetings on the spot, discuss future projects, or both? Will you work to create new associations to broaden your network? Will to try to access and serve leadership teams? All of these are very worthwhile goals. Choose one or two to focus on and be prepared for a well-timed introduction to get you the results you are looking for.

Growth by Associations

I used to go to just about every networking event. I was involved with many associations (and still am). People are so used to seeing me that, even when I don't go places, they assume I was there!

You *are* your associations. Be involved with the associations that pertain to your line of business and be the face of those associations. When I was starting to look into developing my engineering firm, I went to a local agency meeting. As I was walking into the meeting, a lady asked me my name and about my shoes. We started to talk, and I soon found out about NABWIC (National Association for Black Women in Construction). As she shared with me, I realized that this would be an important group for me. She invited me to a meeting that evening and I met the rest of the group. I also met the founder, Ann McNeil, and realized that she was very experienced and totally committed to the cause. She shared her vision and the organization's mission with me.

I decided to go to Miami to experience the meetings in person. I was sold. I asked many questions and started a new chapter where I live in Tampa, Florida. I love to serve, be present for, and be with an association that opens the horizon for many women who have never seen another woman wear a hard hat. These women now have confidence that there is something sexy to that look! Going to local schools, we share the vision, the mission, and the possibilities they create. Almost every little girl has seen a man wearing a hard hat at a construction site, but they haven't seen many women. Women know how to design, build, and deliver, too.

After that association, I also joined COMTO (The Conference of Minority Transportation Officials). At this association, I am a fit through our Land Surveying department. After all, every road needs to be designed and it first needs surveying. Every property a road is built on must be surveyed first. So, I was able to anticipate what major development was coming to our area and get in front of the big projects.

Networks and associations expand the opportunity to create teams. Every job is built by a team. Teams are chosen by people, and people choose the teams they know, like, and trust. It is my business to become known and get the opportunity to be liked and trusted. Associations are like sororities and fraternities. People in associations recommend each other. And, if you give the most, they will *really* remember you.

When it comes to giving, make sure to put your money where your money will produce for you. The fastest way to develop any business is through professional associations. Expect to pay about $100 to $200 for the memberships. I assure you that when your association involvement results in involvement, you will not regret it. Whatever you do, don't join just to say that you are in that association. Be *in* it. I belong to five professional associations and we have annual meetings, quarterly meetings, and weekly online meetings. I make it my business to have a presence in all they are doing.

Once you are active in an association, it's not time to coast. Now it's time to bring that activity to the next level. Association meetings can sometimes feel tedious. But there is a way to prevent that. Don't get bored, get *on* boards! Boards are the backbone of the organization and fulfill the mission of the organization. Join them. Be active on them. Demonstrate your willingness to be a presence in the association and then ask to be part of the board of directors. Become the go-to person in that association. The credibility you will gain will very likely lead to your business becoming the top business of your kind in your region or state.

Chapter 12

THE TRUTH ABOUT CREDIT

∽⟨⟩⟩⟩⟩∾

We are going to address something a bit controversial, but this is knowledge every entrepreneur must have. To grow your business, you will need to know how to manage your business credit.

Credit means credibility

There is a system called a *credit score*, and it is one of the most important things you will manage in your business—especially if you have a new business. The sought-after score is 700 or above. With a good score, you can request finances for equipment, goods, operating funds, and more. If the bids are close, some groups will choose their contractors based on the company's credit score. It's a way for them to establish that your business is financially stable.

Your business has to have at least three years of existing credit to create a score of its own. Until then, the company will run on your personal credit score. You may be tempted to partner with an existing business just to be able to rely on their credit score, but be mindful. Such decisions could break your business as easily as it could make your business. Watch your financials like a hawk, and open and close doors accordingly.

Some basic information to note:

- Credit unions are the best for some personal loans. They are also a little bit more flexible than commercial banks and will support you if you have a good business plan. You can find examples of good business plans on www.sba.gov.

- For the first three years, the owner of the company must use his or her personal credit score for the business.

- To establish the company's credit, choose vendors that report to credit agencies. National retailers that provide supplies to trades or office supplies are a good place to start. Attach your personal identity to the retailer's credit instrument in the company's name. Then, ask their credit department to move the credit instruments to the company's identity.

Even when you have a relationship with a lender, you have to be careful. I requested a credit card with my local credit union and I was approved right on the spot. I was so excited because a bank credit card will help me increase my credit score. I was told that my payments will be the 10th of every month. I received the card on the 20th and waited to make my first payment. While I was waiting, I checked my credit score. I about had a heart attack! My credit score had dropped 40 points. I had expected it to increase because I had more credit available to me. I called the credit unon and found out the name and information of the CFO. To my surprise, they report to the credit bureau agencies on the 5th. I was floored. How could you report before the payment date? I had many intense conversations with the CFO and customer service. Apparently, members were not aware of what was creating the yo-yo credit report they had. I stood for all ten-thousand members and petitioned that the reporting date change to the 15th of the month.

My point is, handle your financial affairs. When you open a line of credit, check to see what interest will accumulate based is on the project timeline. If you aren't careful, you may be paying more in interest than what you net on the project.

Another way to address a financial need you can't meet is by selling the invoices so that you can take care of your payroll. Now, with that in mind, make sure to negotiate your payment arrangements. If you can wait sixty days after payroll and the work has been done, go for it. I know that I couldn't do that in the beginning. For many business owners, bootstrapping is the best answer to all financial issues at the start. Extending yourself through credit or selling invoices is for growth down the road.

I built a relationship with Tim. He works for a company that lends 80% of the contract value. I can honestly tell you that Tim saved the day. He got me set up on a 1% interest loan and was better than any bank. I passed through five contracted projects; not all of our contracts, just what as many as we needed to get ahead in that situation.

Another aspect to consider is the payment timeline. My contracts require a net-30 invoice payment. That means that my company is supposed to get paid within 30 days of the invoice being sent. So, we invoice every Monday. After the first month, it becomes a regular weekly payment. The terms do not suggest when to submit, only how long it will take. There are other contracts were the client has a special platform to submit payments and they control when it can be done. So, be very careful with payment terms, because, at the end of the day, most businesses pay the outlay for a client's project up front. Also make sure to request any insurance payments in the proposal as part of the compensation.

Pivot

This is very emotional chapter for me, I hope that as I share this experience you can come to some sober and calculated business resolutions.

I've been serving the construction industry for four years. Ultimately, everything I do is to meet the challenges and ups and downs of my business. I gave myself some time to grow the company and be at a steady profit level. Yet, it seemed that something was always happening to undermine my ability to consistently meet my goals. I had to find the problem.

I started with engineering. It was hard to find partners or staff who were loyal or had the level of integrity that the market demanded I bring to the business. After that, I added surveying. For that department, I also hired people and learned many lessons about what not to do with that. I've always been a trainer. I love to train executive teams on inclusion and create trainings for all ages about being, doing and having. I love that. And I've never strayed in my determination to deliver a project on the due date. However, I have yet to see a construction project finish on time. That alone is so frustrating to me that I knew I would need to pivot sooner or later.

After losing a contract that nearly took my company under, that experience pushed me to make the move faster than I expected. What I didn't know is that two years prior, I had positioned myself to do exactly that.

Two years previously, I had decided to add safety supply services to my company because there was no woman-owned business registered in my area that provided the service. I didn't do much with it, but it was a part of my offering. I got supplier agreements with the manufacturers and negotiated a 45-day invoice reimbursement. I had no idea how that would benefit me down the road.

When COVID-19 started and I saw the announcement that stores were closing, I asked my husband to go to the beauty supply store to buy my hair products. He called me as he left the store, excited to say that he got a box of hair relaxer. I though he was joking. We had no idea how long the shutdown was going to last! I asked him to go back and buy enough to last me until December. He understood and went back and picked up all my beauty needs: lashes, relaxer, foundations, and so on.

The next morning, he brought me breakfast in bed and we were talking about the direction that the shutdown was going. He happened to mention that the owner offered him a KN95 mask. I stopped him and asked him to repeat that. He said that after he purchased all my supplies, the guy behind the counter told him that his wife should be "very happy" with him and offered him a mask. I was at that store first thing Monday morning and negotiated to buy masks, gloves, and so on—in bulk. It was from that box of masks that I pulled the fifty surgical masks that I passed on to friends of influence as gifts. But the rest stayed in the box.

As I was getting ready for my day, I asked God, "What am going to do during a shutdown?" I got a call from a wonderful lady to talk about business and the shift that we are going through. I mentioned that I did not know what to do, but I trusted that I would be okay. I mentioned that I had 3,000 gloves, and she said, "I'll buy your gloves from you." After that, everyone that I gave gloves to as a gift referred me to a friend. I sold masks from the beauty supply store in the hood to hospitals by the thousands, millions of nitrile gloves, and more gowns than I could count. In four months, I pivoted from $850,000 in revenue to several million.

I had become attached to the hard work of building something from nothing. After many betrayals, tears, and sleepless nights (only God, my pillow, and my husband know my heart, here) I now know a life flowing in abundance. I LOVE everything, and I'm attached to nothing. I will be fine.

Many people ask me, "How do you do that? How do you pivot so easily?" The answer is simple: practice, practice, practice. Moving with the military, children growing and moving to create their own lives, preparing for life's moves—that's practice. Real life—and that's the best practice if you are present and paying attention.

Nothing is permanent. Give it your all, expect great things, and great things will happen, even when it doesn't make sense for it to. If you live long enough, you will be able to see the puzzle pieces come together. Every experience I had was necessary to create what I am doing today. Every contract, every process, and all my experience with people got me to where I am. God guided and orchestrated every instrument and every moment. I'm so blessed to be able to bless others. Now I'm importing and suppling major hospitals nationwide.

Chapter 13

WHAT ARE YOU GOING TO DO?

⟶◉◉◉⟵

If you've come this far with this book, I commend you. Many people get motivated and start something, but they rarely finish. Although I am happy you've come this far, I want you to ask yourself something. From what you've read up until now, are you going to implement anything? Or, are you reading this book just to read it?

I say this with much respect to you and with the best wishes for your endeavors: if you're not going to implement what I've taught so far, please don't bury this knowledge that has taken me decades to learn, and give this book to someone who will.

I wish someone had taken the time to guide me. I bought and read so many books trying to find my way and there seems to be nothing in writing about how to actually perform the daily functions of business.

However, if you're intent on changing your life for the better and living a life by your design, I'm so excited for you to read the next chapter. Up until now, sharing my experiences and passing down some knowledge, what I've done has laid the foundation for what I really want to say in the next chapter. So, if you're ready for a mindset shift, turn the page...

Chapter 14

DON'T CALL ME
A MINORITY!

I mentioned earlier how I bristled at the idea that any group of people be called a minority, or lesser than any other group. I also see the experiences I have had in this country with being called "black" as an offshoot of the same mentality.

In other parts of the world, skin color is something that is observed (dark, light, etc.) but not something that defines us. In Latin America, where everyone is a shade of brown, this is especially true. The reality is that this country is becoming, well… darker. The complexion of this nation, literally and figuratively, is changing. If I want success for you and other people who represent diversity in this country, I have to ask you to do one thing.

Stop calling yourself black

Until you stop calling yourself black, no one will stop calling you black. So, what should you call yourself? Well, your parents gave you a name. When you go to other countries, you can feel the energy of freedom when it comes to the race conversation. This is the only country where, even in business, racism is open and systemic. It's quantified, perpetuated and approved by the federal government.

Some organizations are moving to the concept of "Diversity and Inclusion." The rest are stuck on "minority." And that's too bad. But being black is a learned behavior. I understand that the history of this country originally created that expectation. Choice in the matter was removed. That's a horrible truth. But being present in order to experience success also means living in the present. We have choices now about how we behave and who we choose to surround ourselves with. We are only destined to relive history if we choose to. Humans are humans, with the beauty of difference and authenticity.

After the incident at JC Penney's when I found out that, in the US, I wasn't chocolate like I thought, a good friend told me that I needed to "learn to be black" if I wanted to stay here. She advised me to start using black hair products. I will never forget that she loaned me a movie called *Mississippi Burning*. I could only watch ten minutes of it and turned it off. I had nightmares for days. The history is horrific, but when you know better, you do better.

As of the date of this publication, it's 2020, and we still allow ourselves—even in professional circles—to be called a black business. Let us be a business owner, a small company, or even diverse. But black? What is a black business? Do we perform less? Are we less able? Less professional? A degree does not cost us less just because we may represent a diverse culture. We didn't have to take different tests in school. We had to learn and earn our skills right alongside everyone else.

My son learned that he was black on the first day of school. He came home and said to me, "Mom, some kids call me a 'black boy' at school." Boy, oh boy, was I livid.

I remember going to the mirror with him and asking him: "How many eyes do you have? How many fingers and noses?" I looked him in the eye and said, "You have the same amount as the people who called you that. What color was their skin?" He said pink. I said, "Okay. Because people call you something outside of your name does not make you that. That's why they are in school—to get educated and stop being ignorant."

The rest of that conversation was exceedingly difficult. We are not only considered black, we are Latinos and have a foreign accent. We are from Central America. We always knew that we were Americans. Then I discovered that most North Americans think they are the only Americans. That's funny. But the term "minority" when addressing people is a real insult. I'm a minority to nothing.

Imagine the systemic discrimination inherent in the fact that we have "minority meetings" held by big companies. Who goes to an event for minorities? At my house, we acknowledge the social norm that there are four major people groups: Europeans, Africans, Latinos and Asians. And, yes, we are all descended from one or more of those. It would never cross our mind to call someone a minority. The minority vote never wins, but I'm a winner so I'm not a minority.

Project to others that you are a human being. Minorities don't feel celebrated, they feel tolerated. I refuse to stand for that. As I came into the world of owning my own business, I discovered that if I want to win, I have to be certified as a minority—with my own number. Whoopee. That is the biggest bias I have ever heard of.

I am on a "Diversity and Inclusion" terminology crusade. I am here to tell you that, from my perspective, the word "minority" is everything. I have been in more meetings than I'd like to admit where chocolate Americans ask, "What is the percentage of minorities for the project?" What? That's how brainwashed we are. We look for the handout. We are professionals. The registration and everything else that it takes to set up a company requires the same amount of work and investment from each race.

The word "minority" has been used to represent a small group of people. Throughout the previous generations, we have evolved from Negro to People of Color to African-Americans.

The latter at least addresses a place of origin. But "minority" says nothing useful, nothing helpful, to the people it labels.

I hope you can find your power and support this change. We cannot be called minority anymore. "Diversity and Inclusion" are positive words and do not limit the amount of small or diverse companies that are allowed to provide professional services or delivery of goods. *And, please don't tell me what black is "supposed" to be.* I don't buy the narrative on how "black" people are supposed to be one way or another. Chances are, when left up to someone else to define, it's negative. And that impacts us. As a result, we now define ourselves negatively.

We don't watch BET network in my home. I don't want to see any subliminal messaging teaching us to blame the system and take our hope away so that we stop advancing. Television shows portray black men in business as cheaters, loose and enraged; poor black men as thieves, dirty and unruled. The rest are "in the struggle."

I work with some amazing African-Americans, super-achievers like Brian Butler. I asked Brian recently, before he went to NPR, about his experience as a black man in this country. Since he is well-traveled and has lived abroad, I thought he might have some good insight. I wasn't disappointed. He shared with me the unique challenges of being a "black man" in this country. An educated officer in the military, a passionate advocate for education, he even formed a coalition through one of the biggest counties in Florida. He has advocated for all small business owners to go to every elementary school, visit each classroom, and share about their business and how to be successful. Yet, even as a great business owner, the color of his skin has almost gotten him killed.

I spent some time talking to the chief of the local police department, and he shared how, when he was on vacation with his wife (a lawyer by profession), he was stopped by the police because he was profiled. Behind every human being there is a mother, a father, and a friend, waiting to see them and hear from them. Every person has immense value. Don't allow yourself to be called a minority!

You've heard the expression, "As a man thinketh, so is he." If you feel that you're less than someone, you are. If you feel you are on an equal footing with someone, you are. If you feel that you are blessed and more highly favored than most people, you are. No one can tell you what your limits are but you.

Where is PMS?

Growing up Latina, I never knew I could throw a tantrum and blame it on PMS.

Soon after I came to this country, I went to the bank and there was a lady there who was not happy. She was so upset when she found out that her account had been wiped out by her husband. She lost it with the teller who was, of course, just the messenger. I would have been upset, too, but this woman was out of control. The woman behind me said, "She's probably going through PMS." I had no idea what she was referring to, but I definitely wanted to avoid that place. So, I asked, "What road is that on?" She never answered. I looked up PMS and it is real, but if you don't know that you can have something, you just don't.

I didn't grow up being allowed to make excuses for my behavior. Women were always attentive to their families; we didn't act crazy once a month with people or our loved ones. We worked, cleaned, cooked, and acted normally. It is amazing how different you behave if you don't know you can act better or have an excuse to act silly.

In Latin America, when a woman is depressed or acts crazy, she got three choices: she can go see a doctor; if she was depressed, she needed to get a job; or, if she feel crazy, she needed to get to church for an exorcism where we prayed the devil out of them. Acting crazy isn't something we wanted to do, and hurting or offending others because you're feeling crazy, in our culture, is just not acceptable. So, we didn't.

When you are running a business, you don't get to have PMS or go through it. If you are concerned you won't be able to control your bad behavior, it's better to work from home that day. Every minute counts. You can't lose it and then recall it with an excuse.

While thinking about this topic, I called my 95-year-old grandmother and asked her if she knew what PMS was? She said that she had never heard of that food before. My point is, people don't normally work with nuts!

How you define yourself should be your choice. Don't let others label you or your behavior in a way that lessens you or disempowers you. Take back control. Correct them. Tell them how you want to be defined. Many of you are diverse. Many of you are women. All of you are precious and capable of greatness. Don't listen to anyone who implies anything else.

Chapter 15

CAN YOU IMAGINE?

⁓ↈↈ⁓

Close your eyes and fly with me

Now that you've gotten to the last chapter, I'd like to do a cool exercise with you. I want you to imagine your life twelve months from now. Imagine that you've taken the advice I've given in this book. What does your life look like now?

o You have joined some associations

o You have partnered with bigger companies

o You tell time what to do

o You're on the board of several nonprofits, rubbing shoulders with big-time donors

o You refuse to believe that you're a minority

o You're taking advantage of the "disadvantage" of being

labeled a minority

o   You haven't said "no" to opportunities and found solutions

o   You've been at the right places at the right times

o   You've learned to leverage good credit

o   You've owned up to your mistakes with transparency

o   You're stable and act accordingly with yourself and your business

o   You understand who you are and believe it!

Now, close your eyes and let your imagination take you to where you are in twelve months. Most likely, your life is totally transformed. You're better respected. Important people now seek you out. You have an army of people who know you, like you, and trust you enough that they all refer business to you.

Isn't that the life you want? If the answer is yes, remember that no one can stop you from getting it but you.

You are not alone

Many of us have struggled through some of our worst moments in business only to come out on the other side wiser and more successful. Hang in there. I am reminded of my successes every time I open my linen closet and see the many thick, lush, towels in all my favorite colors. I never wanted to have to share a towel again and I never will. The rewards of success are worth every moment it takes to get there.

You have taken a major step in reading this book, but the breakthrough comes in the execution. If you need further counsel, I'd love to connect with you. I am also available to speak to your event or provide consultation to you or your group.

You can find me at www.vividpros.com. Stay in touch with me so I can continue to provide value to you.

Now that you have finished this book, who else do you know that can benefit from it? Please feel free to gift it away and be a blessing to someone else so that you are *always in service*!

Acknowledgements

Thank you to my children, who taught me to love unconditionally. My Eric, the reason why I get to fly. The many associations that I serve and am served by. The one and only NABWIC (National Association of Black Woman in Construction), its founder, Ann McNeil (mentor and great achiever). To the people of Tampa and the many servants who took the time to show me the way and always believed in me. The many friends who listened to me when I needed an ear, thank you. The one and only for whom I live and breathe and has been my God all along.

About the Author

Mercedes Young is originally from Panama where she obtained her bachelor's degree in Psychology. After over a decade working for the US Department of Defense, she relocated to the United States and began a career in business development serving growing entrepreneurs. With loving support from her husband Eric and her two children, Mercedes launched her civil engineering, land surveying and safety supply company. She also developed and manages Vivid Consulting Group, LLC.

Mercedes serves in many national, state and local associations, including NABWIC (National Association of Black Women In Construction) where she is a national board member, chair for the local marketing and communication for COMTO (Conference of Minority Transportation Officials), member of HPWA (Hispanic Professional Woman Association) leading their "Master Mind" organization. Mercedes is also a graduate of the SBA's Accelerated Leadership Program, an honoree for Prospera (the Hispanic SBA), and she recently accepted a board position on the Latin Chamber of Commerce. Her history represents the fulfillment of her motto "Always in Service."